Cornerstones of Freedom

The Story of
THE CHICAGO FIRE

By R. Conrad Stein

Illustrated by Richard Wahl

 CHILDRENS PRESS, CHICAGO

Library of Congress Cataloging in Publication Data

Stein, R. Conrad.
  The story of the Chicago fire.

  (Cornerstones of freedom)
  Summary: Presents eyewitness accounts of the
devastating effects of the 1871 Chicago fire
and describes the subsequent rebuilding of
the city.
  1. Chicago (Ill.) — Fire, 1871 — Juvenile
literature. [1. Chicago (Ill.) — Fire, 1871]
I. Wahl, Richard, ill. II Title. III. Series.
F548.42.S77   977.3'11041   81-15543
ISBN 0-516-04633-0   AACR2

In September, 1871, thirty businessmen met in a club in downtown Chicago. They had come to Chicago only seven or eight years earlier. Most had only a few dollars in their pockets when they arrived. Now all of them were wealthy.

One of the businessmen rose and held up a glass. He said, "To Chicago—the city that made us all rich."

The others stood and champagne glasses clinked. "To Chicago—the city that made us all rich," they repeated.

Not one of the businessmen guessed that they would soon meet again. Their next meeting would be under very different circumstances.

A month later, another Chicagoan walked down De Koven Street. Dennis Sullivan was on his way to the O'Leary house. Upon arriving, Mr. Sullivan saw no lights inside the house. It was nine o'clock on a Sunday evening. Sullivan guessed that his friends had gone to bed early. So he turned to go home. But something caught his eye. A glow flickered behind the O'Leary house. It came from the barn where Mrs. O'Leary kept six cows and a horse. Mr.

Sullivan stepped closer. Fire! The back of the O'Leary barn was on fire.

Sullivan banged on the windows of the O'Leary house. "Wake up in there," he cried. "Your barn's on fire!"

Other people on the sidewalk heard the commotion. Then they saw orange flames licking up the side of the barn.

"Fire!" shouted a woman. "There's a fire on De Koven Street!"

Shouts echoed down the street. Soon most of the neighborhood knew that a fire was blazing at the O'Leary barn. Children ran to see the new fire. But most people sighed and said to themselves, "Just another fire." It had been a dry summer and many fires had broken out.

No one realized that this fire would be different. It would be a monster. Within twenty-four hours it would turn a mighty city into a pile of ashes.

The Great Chicago Fire started at the O'Leary barn on October 8, 1871. It was a date Chicagoans would always remember. It seemed impossible that one fire could so completely destroy their city. Chicago had been so lucky. Its growth had been spectacular.

Forty years before the fire, Chicago was a soggy marshland. Only a few log cabins marked the site of the future city. They stood on the banks of the Chicago River where it flowed into Lake Michigan. But farmers would soon settle on the Great Plains to the west. Eventually those farmers would feed the people in the big eastern cities. Chicago was a perfect midway point between Great Plains farmers and their markets in the east.

Chicago became the fastest-growing city the world had ever seen. By the end of the Civil War, Chicago was the most important railroad, grain, and livestock city in the country. It was also a city of broad parks and splendid buildings. A new park on the north lakefront was named after President Abraham Lincoln. In the middle of downtown stood

a huge domed courthouse. It had a bell that could be heard from one side of the city to the other. North of downtown was a new water-pumping station. The tower of the pumping station rose gracefully into the sky. Its design made the Water Tower look like a castle.

By 1870, 300,000 people lived in Chicago. Its beauty, its wealth, and its rapid growth astonished the world.

But spreading out from downtown were miserable slums. Houses in the slums had grown just as rapidly as Chicago had grown. The houses were made entirely of wood. Many had been hammered together in less than a week. Connecting the wooden houses were sidewalks made of wood. Below the sidewalks were streets paved with wood.

Everyone knew that these wooden slums were tinderboxes. They could very easily go up in flames. Newspapers warned that a great fire could strike Chicago. The most startling warning came from a famous lecturer named George Francis Train. Train used to give speeches in various American cities. Some people claimed that he had the ability to see into the future. The very day before the fire started, Mr. Train had spoken to a downtown audience. "This is the last public address that will be delivered within these walls," he had said. "A terrible calamity is impending over the city of Chicago! More I cannot say; more I dare not utter."

The small blaze at the O'Leary barn grew. It soon became a pillar of fire that reached high into the night sky. In faraway downtown, a man on a

watchtower spotted the flames. The watchtower stood on top of the courthouse, the tallest building in the city. The man was a fire lookout. His job was to spot fires. When he saw one, he would telegraph its location to the city firehouses.

The lookout clicked out the message to four fire-houses. He said the flames were on the South Side of the city. He was wrong. The fire was actually on the South*west* Side of the city. The lookout sent the fire-men a mile off course. It was a human error, but it was deadly. It gave the fire extra time to catch hold. Even today, fire fighters insist that the best time to stop a fire is during the first few minutes.

Out of the firehouses rumbled the horse-drawn fire engines. Their bells rang wildly as they raced down the streets.

Manning the fire engines were exhausted Chicago firemen. No fireman could remember a worse summer. For two months no heavy rains had fallen. It seemed as if a new fire broke out every few hours. The firemen had answered forty alarms the previous week. Just the day before, the entire department had battled a blaze on the West Side. It had leveled four square blocks. The firemen had fought that fire for fifteen hours. Now once more the men clung to their engines and raced into the night. Many had not slept for two days.

The firemen arrived in the South Side neighborhood where they expected to find the fire. Instead they found only dark streets. They did not realize the fire lookout had sent them to the wrong location.

Then one fireman looked toward the west. He stumbled backward. "Look," he said, pointing.

The sky glowed red and orange. It was the eeriest light any of the men had ever seen. They turned their wagons and headed toward the glow. One fireman said, "It looks like the devil's own fire."

The forces of nature seemed to be on the side of the fire that night. A hot dry wind whipped out of the prairies. It raced over the flatlands of Chicago toward the lake. Driven by the wind, the fire roared toward the heart of the city. Some witnesses later claimed that it traveled as fast as a man can run.

The tinderbox wooden neighborhoods went up first. The fire jumped from one house to the next. It whooshed down the wooden sidewalks and the wood-paved streets. The raging fire swallowed up everything in its path. And it grew as it fed.

People streamed out of the slum houses. Most of them carried a few possessions. They had a single thought. Cross the bridges and escape. Go downtown. Perhaps the fire would not be able to cross the Chicago River. Also, many of the downtown buildings were built of brick. They should be safe from the fire.

As the people ran, they heard the courthouse bell chiming ahead of them. The bell was the city's fire alarm. Men on the watchtower now rang it constantly. To the people fleeing the fire it sounded like the bell on the gates of heaven. Behind them roared the flames of hell.

Most of the people were fast enough to keep ahead of the fire. Some were not. The monster fire swallowed up more than just houses. It killed people, too. Some of the slum dwellers on the Southwest Side were its first victims.

Soon all of Chicago's firemen were battling the blaze. But the city's fire department was badly undermanned. Chicago had only 250 fire fighters and 17 fire engines.

As the fire raced toward downtown, the city fire chief declared it officially out of control. The time was 10:30 P.M. The fire had started only an hour and a half earlier.

A strange orange glow lit up the entire southern end of the city. Still many Chicagoans thought they were safe. The people who lived downtown thought the fire would not reach them. None of the big fires had ever spread as far as downtown. North Siders felt safe, too. In order to reach the North Side, the fire would have to burn up all of downtown. That could never happen, thought the North Siders.

Wild confusion reigned at the south branch of the Chicago River. Thousands of people streamed across the bridges. Horses and wagons tried to push through the crowds. All hoped to reach downtown and safety.

Raging and roaring, the fire pushed up to the river. The river was about as wide as half the length of a football field. At the bank, the fire sent a storm of red-hot cinders raining into the buildings on the other side. Next the bridges themselves caught fire. In minutes, the fire jumped the river and entered downtown.

The courthouse bell continued to ring. But when

the fire swept into downtown, the bell suddenly sounded more urgent.

Some people in the city owned cameras in 1871. But not one photograph of the fire survives. Perhaps the fire moved too quickly to be photographed by the clumsy equipment of the times. Many letters written by eyewitnesses have survived, though. Those letters describe the fear and confusion in Chicago on that terrible night.

Newspaper editor Horace White was struck by how quickly the fire spread down the streets: "The fire was moving northward like ocean surf on a sand beach. . . . A column of flame would shoot up from a burning building, catch the force of the wind, and strike the next one. . . . It was simply indescribable in its terrible grandeur."

Another eyewitness described how animals panicked in the streets: "The horses, maddened by the heat and noise, and irritated by the falling sparks, neighed and screamed with fright and anger, and roared and kicked and bit each other. . . . Dogs ran hither and thither, howling dismally. Great brown rats, with beadlike eyes, were ferreted out from under the sidewalks by the flames, and scurried down the streets."

A high school principal wrote about the sheer power of the fire: "The long tongues of flame would dart out over a whole block, then come back and lap it all clean. Iron and stone seemed to come down as if in a blast furnace."

In the panic of the fire some people became criminals. Others became heroes.

When the fire threatened the county jail, the jailors released three hundred prisoners. Those prisoners ran gleefully into the streets. Many of them immediately looked for something to steal.

Looting broke out when police had to abandon endangered streets. Visiting New Yorker Alexander Frear wrote, "Lake Street was rich with treasure and hordes of thieves forced their way into the stores and flung out merchandise to their fellows in the streets, who received it without disguise and fought for it openly."

Liquor stores were a main target for the looters. Mr. Frear described this street-corner scene: "A fellow standing on a piano declared that the fire was the friend of the poor man. He wanted everyone to help himself to the best liquor he could get, and continued to yell from the piano until someone as drunk as himself flung a bottle at him...."

Many of the looters became victims of their own greed. Some tried to carry off too much. They later had to abandon their goods or be overcome by the advancing fire. Others died when the fire swept over the buildings from which they were stealing.

But for every looter there were dozens of heroes.

Reports told of men and women rushing bravely into burning buildings to rescue others who were trapped. Many people abandoned their household goods so they could carry injured persons to safety.

Owners of horse-and-wagon teams (called cartmen) carried many people and goods away from the fire. Newspaper editor Horace White wrote, "I saw a great many kindly acts done as we moved along. The poor helped the rich and the rich helped the poor (if anyone could be called rich at such a time).... I heard of cartmen demanding one hundred and fifty dollars (in hand, of course) for carrying a single load. Very likely it was so, but those cases did not come under my notice. It did come under my notice that some cartmen worked for whatever the sufferer felt able to pay, and one I knew worked for nothing."

In the very center of downtown stood the splendid

courthouse building. Its great bell pealed through the smoky night. The building symbolized old Chicago. It was often seen on picture postcards of the city. During the height of the fire an eyewitness described this scene at the courthouse: "The Courthouse Park was filled with people, who appeared to be huddled together in a solid mass, helpless and astounded. The whole air was lit with falling cinders, and it looked like a snowstorm lit by colored fire."

Firemen hosed water on the courthouse. But flaming cinders rained down on its roof. Soon the famous building caught fire. People in the courthouse park fled. As the flames roared upward, the great bell on the tower broke loose. It crashed through five floors before pounding into the basement. People claimed that the great bell was pealing to the end.

One by one, other famous buildings fell to the fire. The Grand Pacific Hotel was destroyed. It had one of the first elevators Chicagoans had ever seen. The elevator was described as "a vertical railroad to connect all floors." The fire razed the elegant Field and Leiter's store. It had been advertised as "two million dollars of marble magnificence." The owners of the *Chicago Tribune* had called their building "com-

pletely fireproof." It burned to the ground in a little more than an hour.

Many of these structures were soundly built. But the heat of this fire could destroy anything. Solid iron light posts were melted down to half their size. Sometimes the fire seemed to sculpt those light posts. It molded the posts into eerie figures that looked strangely like terrified men and women. The furnacelike heat was so intense that it melted the iron wheels of railroad cars. It turned railroad tracks into long twisting snakes.

Early Monday morning while the fire still raged, a group of businessmen met in a restaurant. The same group had met a month earlier to toast their success. They had been poor men who grew rich in booming Chicago. Now each of them was poor once again. Overnight they had lost all they owned.

One of the men passed out glasses and poured champagne. He held his glass high and said, "To Chicago—the city that made us rich, and then busted us."

The men rose and champagne glasses clinked. Each man smiled grimly. Although they had lost everything, they still felt lucky just to be alive. The men were not able to finish their toast. The restaurant they were in caught fire. The men rushed outside carrying their champagne with them. They finally finished the bottle on the shores of Lake Michigan.

One businessman actually made money because of the fire. John Drake owned the Tremont Hotel. When the fire threatened his hotel, Mr. Drake told his guests to leave. He then abandoned the hotel. He did not even bother to close the front door. He walked east toward the newly built Avenue Hotel. He had a hunch. Perhaps the fire would not come this far east. Drake walked into the Avenue Hotel. He offered to buy it for a fraction of its worth. Drake put one thousand dollars cash on the owner's desk as a down payment. The owner agreed to sell, thinking his hotel would soon be destroyed by the fire. Strangely, the fire never entered the southeast section of downtown Chicago. The Avenue Hotel remained undamaged. John Drake had bought one of Chicago's finest hotels for next to nothing.

On Monday, October 9, units of the United States Army moved into Chicago. The army planned to blow up a strip of buildings. They hoped to blast open a gap so wide the fire could not cross it. Their efforts failed. The fire spread too quickly. The soldiers did not even have time to set up their dynamite. Besides, this fire could probably have crossed any gap.

The monster fire soon jumped the main branch of the Chicago River. Then it roared into the North Side. North Siders had had more time to prepare to abandon their homes. Many of them buried their valuables in their front yards. Some reports told of families burying grand pianos in their front yards.

Thousands of people, fleeing the fire, headed for the cool waters of Lake Michigan. There they gathered at the new park named after President Lincoln. Today, Chicago's Lincoln Park is one of the loveliest city parks anywhere in the world. In 1871, however, an old cemetery still covered many acres of the park. When the fire struck, city workers had been digging up the old graves to make way for the park. The workers were moving the graves to a cemetery farther north. During the fire, many Chicagoans huddled in the freshly dug-up graves. Others walked off the beaches and stood neck high in the water. Men drove horses and wagons directly into the lake. People and animals bobbed like apples off the shores of Lake Michigan.

A brave woman named Aurelia King described what it was like to escape the fire by running to Lincoln Park: "I fled with my children clinging to me, fled literally in a shower of fire. . . . The wind was like a tornado and I held fast to my little ones, fearing they would be lifted from my sight. . . . On and on we ran till we entered Lincoln Park. There among the empty graves of the old cemetery we finally sat down."

Masses of people huddled together in Lincoln Park. There they waited for some force of nature to weaken the fire. Perhaps a wind would blow in the opposite direction. Perhaps there would be a drop of rain. Anything would help.

Hours dragged on while the fire raged. Many people wept as they saw their city go up in flames. Others prayed. On the shores of Lake Michigan some of the injured people died as they waited for a break in the fire.

Suddenly a man in Lincoln Park shouted, "Look, I can see the Water Tower." The man pointed. "Look there! The Water Tower is still standing."

People strained to look. Through the smoke they saw the new Water Tower. It stood tall and proud. Neighboring buildings had been flattened. But the

Water Tower defied the monster fire. The sight of that tower filled the people with courage. If the Water Tower can survive this fire, we can too, they thought. Again someone shouted, "The Water Tower is still standing." Others picked up the shout. "The Water Tower is still standing. The Water Tower is still standing!"

Finally, at ten o'clock on Monday evening, a rain began to fall. That rain began to weaken the power of the monster fire. The rain was the answer to one hundred thousand prayers.

The fire smoldered for the next two days. Certainly the most damage had been done during the first terrible twenty-four hours. According to the records, the last building destroyed was a doctor's house on Fullerton Street. That was in the northernmost section of the city. The fire had swept from the South Side to the North Side, destroying everything in its path.

Investigations were begun to determine the cause of the fire. But little was learned. It was concluded only that the fire started in the O'Leary barn—and that Dennis Sullivan was the first to spot the flames. For over a century, a popular Chicago legend held that the fire started when one of Mrs. O'Leary's cows kicked over a kerosene lamp. But from the beginning, Mrs. O'Leary claimed there was no kerosene lamp in the barn that night. One of the O'Leary sons later said the fire started because some boys were smoking a pipe in the barn's hayloft. Another story was that Dennis Sullivan started the fire himself. Mr. Sullivan liked to drink whiskey, and he could have been careless with a match.

No one will ever know the exact cause of the Chicago Fire.

Amid the ashes of their city, Chicagoans counted

their losses. Three hundred people were dead, hundreds had been injured, and many thousands were homeless. Four square miles of homes and other buildings had burned to the ground. Property losses were put at two hundred million dollars.

While smoke still curled into the sky, John Greenleaf Whittier wrote a poem about the Chicago Fire. One stanza ended with these lines:

> Men clasped each other's hands and said
> "The City of the West is dead."

But Chicago was not dead. The fire was still smoldering when one businessman put a sign over the ruins of his office. The sign read, "All gone, but wife, children, and energy!" In its first issue after the fire, the *Chicago Tribune* said, "Chicago still exists. She was not a mere collection of stone, and brick, and lumber."

After the fire, Chicago sprang to life like the strange bird called the phoenix. In ancient Egyptian mythology, the phoenix was a huge bird that once lived in the Arabian desert. Suddenly the phoenix burst into flames and died. Then it rose from its own ashes to start a new life. Chicago, too, rose from its own ashes. It soared into the sky like the mythical bird called the phoenix.

With breathtaking speed Chicagoans rebuilt their city. The rebuilding project became an adventure. Young architects from all over the world flocked to the city. One of those architects was Louis Sullivan. Sullivan and others started the "Chicago School" of architecture. Chicago School architects designed buildings using new materials. These buildings were held up by steel instead of brick. They were light and airy and had bands of windows wrapping around each floor. Because these buildings used the newly developed elevator, they soared eight, nine, and ten stories into the sky.

In 1874 a British visitor walked on State Street in the middle of downtown Chicago. He wrote, "It is difficult to realize the fact that the busy thoroughfare with its beautiful buildings. . . was but three years before a heap of charred ruins."

Today Chicago remains a thriving city. Visitors are still impressed by its richness and beauty.

Southwest of busy downtown there now stands a large bronze sculpture of a flame. It symbolizes the fury of the great fire of 1871. The sculpture rises at the spot where Mrs. O'Leary's barn once stood. Behind the sculpture is the Chicago Fire Academy. It is the building where today's beginning fire fighters are trained.

On the northern end of downtown stands another symbol of the Chicago Fire. Amid glittering office buildings, the Water Tower rises gracefully above Michigan Avenue. It is the same building that defied the great fire. Thousands of Chicagoans saw the Water Tower through the smoke on that October day more than one hundred years ago. The image of the tower filled the people with courage. That courage gave Chicagoans the strength to rebuild their great city.

About the Author

R. Conrad Stein was born and grew up in Chicago. He attended the University of Illinois, where he earned a degree in history. He later studied at the University of Guanajuato in Mexico.

History is Mr. Stein's hobby. He is especially interested in the history of the city of Chicago. He was delighted when Childrens Press asked him to write this book about the Chicago Fire.

Mr. Stein is married to Deborah Kent, who is also a writer of books for young readers.

About the Artist

Richard Wahl, graduate of the Art Center College of Design in Los Angeles, has illustrated a number of magazine articles and books. He is a skilled artist and photographer who advocates realistic interpretations of his subjects. He lives with his wife and two sons in Louisville, Kentucky.